VFR ATC COMMUNICATIONS

ISBN: 1500386103
ISBN-13: 978-1500386108
V: 12

AIR TRAFFIC CONTROL:

> *"Cessna Five-Six-Two-Mike Papa, say altitude."*

STUDENT PILOT:

> *"Altitude!... Two-Mike-Papa."*

TABLE OF CONTENTS

INTRODUCTION

Communication can be a daunting and scary task for a new pilot. The key to making communication easy is to become prepared with all forms of communication, whether it's pilot-to-pilot or controller-to-pilot. This guide will help you to prepare for all forms of VFR communication.

After you have become familiar with all phrases and scenarios, you must muster up the courage to communicate because the only way to become a great aviation communicator is to practice, practice, practice!

One of the key elements of piloting is resource management. That is to say, pilots should always use all available resources to them in order to conduct a safe and efficient flight. In this case, a new pilot should use any resource available to them in order to become more familiar with radio communication. If you can afford it, purchasing and monitoring a handheld radio (e.g. a transceiver or scanner) will quickly enhance your abilities to communicate, not to mention a handheld transceiver is a great tool to have in case of a radio failure.

Another great resource is the internet. www.LiveATC.net is a great website that provides live feeds from many national and international airport towers and control centers.

HOW TO USE THIS GUIDE

This guide was primarily developed for those who are learning how to fly, and so it is structured in such a way to be useful for a new student pilot. Phase I discusses all the basic communication required to fly in and out of a controlled or uncontrolled airport. Furthermore, new pilots should take a look at Appendix A for a better understanding of ATIS/AWOS/ASOS.

Phase II of this book discusses advanced communication that is typically used during the en-route phase of a flight. If you are just learning to fly, this communication will typically only be used during the second half of your flight training. In any case, new pilots should attempt to become familiar with all forms of communication as soon as practicable. So if you're ready to become an excellent aviation communicator, give this book a read in its entirety... roger that?

PHASE I

THE BASICS

PHONETIC ALPHABET

A – Alpha	B – Bravo	C – Charlie
D – Delta	E – Echo	F – Foxtrot
G – Golf	H – Hotel	I – India
J – Juliet	K – Kilo	L – Lima
M – Mike	N –November	O – Oscar
P – Papa	Q – Quebec	R – Romeo
S – Sierra	T – Tango	U – Uniform
V – Victor	W – Whiskey	X – X-ray
Y – Yankee	Z – Zulu	

RUNWAYS AND TAXIWAYS

19L – One Niner Left (NOT "nineteen left")

F D – Foxtrot Delta (NOT "eff, dee")

25L @ D – Two Five Left at Delta

ALTITUDES

1,500 – One thousand five hundred (NOT "fifteen hundred")

4,500 – Four thousand five hundred

11,500 – One–one thousand, five hundred (NOT "eleven thousand…")

CALL SIGNS

N562MP – Five Six Two Mike Papa (the "November" at the beginning is optional). The call sign may be shortened to the last 3 alphanumeric characters only once ATC has done so.

DEFINITIONS (PART I)

ATIS – Automated Terminal Information Service. This is a looped recording at controlled airports, updated every hour of operation (typically 5 minute prior to the top of the hour). ATIS reports the airport weather, as well as airport information (e.g., NOTAMs). Every time ATIS changes, it will be assigned a different code (e.g., Alpha, Bravo, Charlie, etc.). This code will be used to advise ground or tower that you have received the ATIS information.

AWOS – Automated Weather Observation System. Similar to ATIS, however there is no code because it is typically only located at uncontrolled airports. The looped recording will have a digitized voice.

ASOS – Automated Surface Observation System. Similar to AWOS, ASOS is a newer system which can provide further details on the weather (i.e., precipitation details, thunderstorm information).

CLEARANCE DELIVERY (AKA "Clearance") – This is a person you communicate with at large airports (Can be found in class B, C, and some D airspaces). Their primary focus is to give IFR aircraft a "clearance." For the bigger airports (usually only B and C airspace airport), VFR aircraft must also get a clearance to depart the area. A VFR clearance will be simple, short instructions on how to depart their airspace (e.g., heading to fly, transponder squawk code, etc.).

GROUND CONTROL (AKA "Ground") – Ground control is only at controlled airports and it is through them that you get permission to taxi throughout the airport, whether it is to the runway, to parking, or to the fuel pit. Their instructions must be followed and read back verbatim.

TOWER – Tower is in charge of the airplanes using, or about to use, the runway. In some instances, ground control may provide clearance to cross a runway, but tower is in charge of every other operation on the runway. The tower gives aircraft clearance to land and takeoff, amongst other things (e.g., airspace transitions, etc.).

COMMUNICATING

During initial contact with any type of controller—or when making calls on a Common Traffic Advisory Frequency (CTAF)—the pilot must always state the following in such order:

1. Who THEY Are (Who you are calling)
2. Who YOU are (Your tail number or call sign)
3. WHERE you're at (location on the ground or in the air)
4. WHAT you want (Your request and/or intentions)

EXAMPLE 1
(1) Long Beach Tower
(2) Cessna 1–1–8–0–2
(3) Holding short of 2–5–Left at Delta
(4) Request straight out departure

EXAMPLE 2
(1) Las Vegas Ground
(2) Columbia 2–2–5–Kilo–Whiskey
(3) At Signature
(4) Ready to taxi to runway 1–9–right

EXAMPLE 3
(1) Jacksonville Tower
(2) Cessna 1–1–8–0–2
(3) Clear of 2-6 at hotel
(4) Taxi back to runway 2-6

EXAMPLE 4
(1) Aiken traffic
(2) Columbia 2–2–5–Kilo–Whiskey
(3) 10 miles south
(4) Inbound for left traffic runway 7

Upon receiving a reply, ensure you respond with all the instructions, completing the radio transmission with your full call sign. Only until the controller has addressed you by a shortened call sign (i.e. the last three alphanumeric characters in your call sign) may you reply with the same shortened call sign.

When reading back instructions, it is important to distinguish the difference between <u>information</u>, <u>clearance</u>, <u>questions</u>, and <u>instructions</u>.

INFORMATION – Most information does not necessarily have to be read back. In many cases a simple "Roger (plus the call sign)" will suffice in the reply. One of the few instances where a thorough reply is required with information is when ATC is calling out other traffic. In that case, the pilot should have one of two responses ready: (1) "Traffic in sight" or (2) "Looking for traffic."

CLEARANCE – Clearances should always be read back. This includes, but is not limited to: a VFR departure clearance, a takeoff clearance, a landing clearance, and clearance to enter certain airspace. All clearances should be read back verbatim. If a pilot is cleared to takeoff from runway 2–6–left, then the pilot must reply, "Cleared for takeoff, runway 2–6–left (plus the call sign)." The pilot should never omit the specific runway number.

QUESTIONS – Pilot's should be aware if ATC is asking a question. Many times, questions are formed as a demand (i.e. "Say altitude"). Furthermore, yes or no questions should be answered with either "affirmative" or "negative." The word "roger" should NOT be used when answering a yes or no question.

INSTRUCTIONS – Very much like clearances, all instructions MUST be read back in their entirety. Pilots must be capable of distinguishing instructions from anything else. When ATC gives information AND instructions, the pilot may respond with "Roger (for the information part)" followed by the instructions as they were given.

PILOT PHRASES

"ROGER" – This is the equivalent of "OK." It is simply a means of telling ATC that you understand. However, it is often incorrectly used in cases where a "Roger" will not suffice. It should NOT be used when replying to instructions or clearances. It should ONLY be used to reply to information.

"AFFIRMATIVE" – This is the equivalent of saying "yes." This should be used when answering 'yes' to a yes or no question. Pilots should NOT use "roger" when replying to a yes or no question.

"NEGATIVE" – This is the equivalent of saying "no."

"WILCO" –Short for "will comply". <u>Although not proper communications</u>, it is used by pilots to inform ATC that they have received the message, understand it, and will comply with it.

"NO JOY" OR "NEGATIVE CONTACT" – Used by pilots to inform ATC that previously issued traffic is not in sight. **"Looking for traffic"** can be used in lieu of "no joy" or "negative contact."

"VERIFY..." – ATC or pilots are requesting confirmation of information.

"TRAFFIC IN SIGHT" – Used by pilots to inform a controller that previously issued traffic is in sight.

"STUDENT PILOT" – Using this phrase will advise ATC that you are a student pilot; therefore, they should communicate slowly and in simple terms. Pilots who opt to use it should use it on initial contact with every controller.

"SAY AGAIN" – This should be used anytime you need ATC to repeat what they said. Another variation of this is, "please repeat." This should be used anytime a pilot does not understand what ATC said. If only part of the transmission was not understood, then the pilot should repeat the instructions that were understood followed by "say again". ATC will then repeat the portion that you did not repeat back. It may also be a good idea to combine this with "student pilot" so that ATC is careful about repeating slowly. Do NOT be shy about using this. It is vital to understand everything that ATC said and it is MUCH safer if you ask them to repeat rather than pretend you understood.

UNCONTROLLED AIRPORT OPERATIONS

CTAF

The Common Traffic Advisory Frequency (CTAF) is used at uncontrolled airports to allow pilots to make self–announcements to other traffic that may be in the area. Because there is no tower to organize traffic and provide traffic alerts, thorough and clear communication is integral to the safety of flight.

The frequencies used for CTAF at one airport may also be used for another nearby airport. For this reason, pilots should always end each transmission with the name of the airport they are operating in. The reason for this is that another pilot listening on the same frequency may only catch the latter half of the transmission, and therefore, by ending your transmission with the name of the area you are operating in, a pilot listening can determine if you are a factor or not.

PHRASES

"OVERHEAD" OR "OVER THE FIELD" – Implies that you are or will be over the airport. You can also opt to simply say, "over the field" or "over the airport."

"ENTERING ON THE 45" – Implies that you are or will be entering downwind on a 45 degree angle.

"LAST CALL" – Informs the other traffic that you will no longer be making further calls and also implies that you will no longer be monitoring the frequency.

"THE ACTIVE" – This is used to describe the runway that is currently active. Regardless of the fact, pilots should still use the runway numbers when operating at uncontrolled airports.

EXAMPLE 1 (departing)
PILOT – *"French Valley traffic, Cessna 5–6–2–Mike Papa, taking off runway 18 for a right crosswind departure, French Valley."*

...

PILOT – *"French Valley traffic, Cessna 5–6–2–Mike Papa, turning right crosswind 18, French Valley."*

...

PILOT – *"French Valley traffic, Cessna 5–6–2–Mike Papa, 5 miles west, last call, French Valley."*

EXAMPLE 2 (inbound to land)
PILOT – *"French Valley traffic, Cessna 5–6–2–Mike Papa, 10 miles west at 3,000, inbound for left traffic 18, French Valley."*

...

PILOT – *"French Valley traffic, Cessna 5–6–2–Mike Papa, over the field at 3,000, will enter the left traffic for 18 on the 45, French Valley."*

...

PILOT – *"French Valley traffic, Cessna 5–6–2–Mike Papa, at 2,300, inbound on the 45 for left traffic 18, French Valley."*

EXAMPLE 3 (in the traffic pattern)
PILOT – *"Lawrenceville traffic, Cessna 5–6–2–Mike Papa, on the upwind, runway 18, Lawrenceville."*

...

PILOT – *"Lawrenceville traffic, Cessna 5–6–2–Mike Papa, turning left crosswind 18, Lawrenceville."*

...

PILOT – *"Lawrenceville traffic, Cessna 5–6–2–Mike Papa, left downwind, runway 18, Lawrenceville."*

...

PILOT – *"Lawrenceville traffic, Cessna 5–6–2–Mike Papa, left base for runway 18, Lawrenceville."*

...

PILOT – *"Lawrenceville traffic, Cessna 5–6–2–Mike Papa, turning final for 18, Lawrenceville."*

NOTE: Notice that sometimes certain words (e.g., "runway") are omitted to make the transmission more concise. What's important is that all vital information is mentioned during your communications on CTAF.

OBTAINING A VFR CLEARANCE

CLEARANCE DELIVERY

A VFR clearance is required when departing a large airport that has a Clearance Delivery (CD). Because this is the first person you are contacting, you must advise them that you have the current ATIS information.

Some class D airports, such as Long Beach Airport (KLGB), do not require you to obtain a VFR Clearance, though you may still be obligated to contact Clearance Delivery prior to contacting ground.

A thorough VFR clearance will contain 4 vital items. To help in copying the VFR clearance, you should use the "RAFT" mnemonic.
- Route
- Altitude
- Frequency
- Transponder Code

PHRASES

"SAY TYPE AND EQUIPMENT" – ATC is asking you for your type of airplane (e.g., C172, PA28, DA20, etc.) and equipment suffix (e.g., Uniform, Golf, etc.).

"MAINTAIN AT OR ABOVE…" – ATC is asking you to maintain at or above a certain altitude.

"MAINTAIN AT OR BELOW…" – ATC is asking you to maintain at or below a certain altitude.

"SQUAWK" – Activate a specific mode or code on the aircraft transponder.

"STAND BY" – ATC may advise a pilot to stand by, at which point the pilot should await further instructions. Pilots are not required to read back "stand by" instructions.

EXAMPLE 1
Pilot – *"Long Beach Clearance, Cessna 5–6–2–Mike–Papa, @ Signature, Request 2–5–Left @ Delta, with information _(ATIS CODE)_ ."*

CD – *"Cessna 5–6–2–Mike–Papa, Long Beach Clearance, contact ground."*

Pilot – *"Contact ground, Cessna 5–6–2–Mike Papa."*

EXAMPLE 2
Pilot – *"Tulsa Clearance, Cessna 5–6–2–Mike–Papa, @ Atlantic Aviation, VFR departure to the west, with information _(ATIS CODE)_ ."*

CD – *"Cessna 5–6–2–Mike–Papa, Tulsa Clearance, you are cleared out of class charlie, on departure fly runway heading, maintain at or below 3,000, frequency 119.1, squawk 0246."*

Pilot – *"Roger, on departure fly runway heading, maintain at or below 3,000, frequency 119.1, squawk 0246, Cessna 5–6–2–Mike–Papa."*

EXAMPLE 3
PILOT – *"Santa Barbara Clearance, Cessna 5–6–2–Mike Papa, @ Signature, Request VFR Clearance to Las Vegas McCarran at niner thousand five hundred, we are a Cessna 172/G*."*

CD – *"Cessna 5–6–2–Mike Papa, Santa Barbara Clearance, on departure, fly runway heading, maintain at or below 1,500, departure on 120.55, squawk 4–2–4–6."*

PILOT – *"Roger. on departure, fly runway heading, maintain at or below 1,500, departure on 120.55, squawk 4–2–4–6, Cessna 5–6–2–Mike–Papa."*

CD – *"Cessna 5–6–2–Mike–Papa, read back is correct, contact ground for taxi."*

PILOT – *"Contact ground for taxi, Cessna 5–6–2–Mike–Papa."*

EXAMPLE 4

PILOT – *"Las Vegas Clearance, Cessna 5–6–2–Mike Papa, @ Signature, Request VFR Clearance to Long Beach airport at one zero thousand five hundred, we are a Cessna 172/G*."*

CD – *"Stand by…"*

CD – *"Cessna 5–6–2–Mike Papa, Las Vegas Clearance, you are cleared out of class bravo airspace via heading 1–7–5, climb and maintain 5,000, frequency will be 125.9, squawk 4–3–5–6."*

PILOT – *"Roger. Cleared out of class bravo airspace via heading 1–7–5, climb and maintain 5 thousand, frequency 125.9, squawk 4–3–5–6, Cessna 5–6–2–Mike Papa."*

CD – *"Cessna 5–6–2–Mike–Papa, read back is correct, contact ground for taxi."*

PILOT – *"Contact ground for taxi, Cessna 5–6–2–Mike–Papa."*

*Advising clearance of your type and equipment (e.g., C172/G) is required.

GROUND CONTROL

GROUND CONTROL

You must contact ground control at controlled airports when taxiing on a "movement area". This involves, but is not limited to: taxiing to the runway, taxiing to parking, and taxiing to the fuel pit.

It is important to read back ALL instructions. This is especially true for "hold short" instructions

PHRASES

"CROSS" – Ground control MUST clear you to cross all runways that are along your taxi route. Furthermore, ground control can only clear to cross one runway at a time. So, if there are two runways to cross along your taxi route, ground control will have to wait for you to cross the first runway before they can clear you to cross the second runway that is along your taxi route.

"HOLD SHORT" – Ground control may ask you to hold short of a runway or taxiway, typically to allow other aircraft to pass. Pilots are required to read back all hold short instructions, as it is vital for avoiding runway and taxiway incursions.

"BEHIND/FOLLOW" – Ground control may ask you to follow (or go behind) an aircraft that is taxiing down a taxiway that you will be using.

"USE CAUTION" – Ground control may advise you to use caution due to other aircraft, personnel in the airport, or other hazardous conditions.

"PROGRESSIVE TAXI INSTRUCTIONS" – This is a request made by pilots, asking ground control to give you step–by–step taxi instructions (e.g. "turn left at the next taxi way... make a right after passing the C–130... you will see a blue building on your left..."). This is a useful tool for a pilot when they arrive at an unfamiliar airport. Remember, it is always better to be safe than to take a risk and accidentally making a mistake on taxi (e.g. taxiing into an active runway).

EXAMPLE 1 (taxiing to runway)

PILOT – *"Long Beach Ground, Cessna 5–6–2–Mike–Papa, @ Signature, request taxi to runway 2–5–Left @ Delta, with information _(ATIS CODE)_ "*

GND – *"Cessna 5–6–2–Mike–Papa, Long Beach Ground, taxi to runway 2–5–Left @ Delta via Foxtrot, cross runway 3–4–Left."*

PILOT – *"Taxi to runway 2–5–Left @ Delta via Foxtrot, cross runway 3–4–Left, Cessna 5–6–2–Mike Papa."*

EXAMPLE 2 (taxiing to runway)

PILOT – *"Las Vegas Ground, Cessna 5–6–2–Mike–Papa, @ Signature, ready to taxi, with _(ATIS CODE)_ "*

GND – *"Cessna 5–6–2–Mike–Papa, Las Vegas Ground, behind the Citation, taxi to runway 1–9–Right via Hotel."*

PILOT – *"Behind the citation, taxi to runway 1–9–Right via Hotel, Cessna 5–6–2–Mike Papa."*

EXAMPLE 3 (after landing)

PILOT – *"Las Vegas Ground, Cessna 5–6–2–Mike–Papa, clear of runway 1–9–Right, taxi to Signature."*

GND – *"Cessna 5–6–2–Mike–Papa, Las Vegas Ground, taxi to Signature via Sierra and Hotel, use caution for a helicopter on Hotel."*

PILOT – *"Roger, taxi to Signature via Sierra and Hotel, Cessna 5–6–2–Mike Papa."*

TOWER CONTROL

TOWER CONTROL

Tower is in charge of the aircraft taking off and those who are inbound to land. Additionally, tower may control the aircraft that are taxiing and are about to cross runways, and just like ground, all instructions must be read back with your call sign.

When approaching an airport to land, ensure that you receive the weather (e.g. ATIS) information prior to making contact with the tower or CTAF.

Certain airports, though very few of them, are authorized to issue a Land and Hold Short Clearance (LAHSO). This would require the pilot to land and ensure that he/she holds short of a certain intersection. Because of the complexity and skill required, student pilots are not allowed to accept a LAHSO clearance.

PHRASES

"HOLD SHORT" – Ground control may ask you to hold short of a runway or taxiway, typically to allow other aircraft to pass. Pilots are required to read back all hold short instructions, as it is vital for avoiding runway and taxiway incursions.

"LINE UP AND WAIT" – ATC authorization to line up on the runway and wait for a takeoff clearance. This usually takes places while other aircraft or vehicles clear the departure area and/or runway.

"CLEARED FOR TAKEOFF" – ATC authorization for an aircraft to depart.

"NO DELAY" OR "IMMEDIATELY" OR "EXPEDITE" – ATC is requesting you take minimal time in following instructions. This is typically requested when landing or taking off.

"CAUTION WAKE TURBULENCE" – ATC is advising the pilot to exercise caution due to potentially hazardous wake turbulence that is caused by another, usually much larger aircraft.

"SAY RUNWAY REQUEST" –ATC may ask you for the runway you are requesting.

"FLY DIRECT TO..." – ATC is asking you to fly direct to a certain location (e.g., VOR, airport, landmark, etc.). In many cases, tower may ask you to fly direct "to the numbers", which implies you are to fly direct to the arrival end of the runway (where the runway numbers are painted).

"REPORT" – A controller may ask you to report over a certain landmark or when in position in the traffic pattern (e.g., downwind, turning final, etc.).

"MAINTAIN BEST FORWARD SPEED" – The controller is requesting you fly your fastest practical speed. This is usually requested because they will have a faster airplane follow you into the airport.

"MAINTAIN SLOWEST PRACTICAL SPEED" – ATC is requesting you fly your slowest practical speed. This is usually requested because they are providing space between you and other aircraft.

"CLEARED TO LAND" – ATC authorization for an aircraft to land.

"CLEARED FOR THE OPTION" – ATC authorization for an aircraft to make a touch–and–go, low approach, missed approach, stop-and-go, or full stop landing at the discretion of the pilot. It is normally used in training.

"GO AROUND" – Instruction for a pilot to abandon his/her approach to landing. Additional instruction may follow. Unless otherwise advised by ATC, a VFR aircraft should overfly the runway while climbing to traffic pattern altitude and enter the traffic pattern via the crosswind leg.

"MAKE SHORT APPROACH" – ATC may inform a pilot to alter his/her traffic pattern so as to make a short final approach (i.e. turn base leg early).

"IDENT" – ATC is asking the pilot to push the "ident" button on the transponder.

"RECYCLE" – A controller may ask you to recycle your transponder. This means to turn off your transponder and then turn it back on.

"TRAFFIC WILL BE HOLDING IN POSITION" – ATC is informing a pilot that another aircraft will be holding in position on the runway of intended landing or an adjacent runway. To acknowledge, a pilot may reply with "roger".

"TRAFFIC TO FOLLOW IS..." – ATC is advising that the pilot is to follow an aircraft as described by ATC (e.g. "traffic to follow is on 2-mile final"). ATC may also use **"you are following traffic at [location]"** followed by the pilots number in sequence to the runway (e.g. "you are following traffic on base, runway 25, cleared to land, number 2").

"SAY CALL SIGN" – ATC is asking for your call sign.

"SAY ALTITUDE" – ATC is asking for your altitude.

EXAMPLE 1 (departing)

PILOT – *"Long Beach Tower, Cessna 5–6–2–Mike–Papa, holding short of 2–5–Left @ Delta, request a left crosswind departure."*

TWR – *"Cessna 5–6–2–Mike–Papa, Long Beach Tower, left crosswind departure approved, runway 2–5–Left @ Delta cleared for takeoff."*

PILOT – *"Runway 2–5–Left @ Delta cleared for takeoff, Cessna 5–6–2–Mike Papa."*

EXAMPLE 2 (inbound to land)

PILOT – *"Long Beach Tower, Cessna 5–6–2–Mike–Papa, 7 miles South, inbound to land runway 2–5–Left with _ (ATIS CODE) _."*

TWR – *"Cessna 5–6–2–Mike–Papa, Long Beach Tower, make left traffic for runway 2–5–Left, report Signal Hill (landmark)."*

PILOT – *"Make left traffic runway 2–5–Left, report Signal Hill, Cessna 5–6–2–Mike Papa."*

EXAMPLE 3 (hold short instructions)

PILOT – *"Long Beach Tower, Cessna 5–6–2–Mike–Papa, holding short of 2–5–Left @ Delta, request a straight out departure."*

TWR – *"Cessna 5–6–2–Mike–Papa, Long Beach Tower, hold short of 2–5–Left, landing traffic."*

PILOT – *"Roger, hold short of runway 2–5–Left @ Delta, Cessna 5–6–2–Mike Papa."*

EXAMPLE 4 (departing–staying in the traffic pattern)

PILOT – *"Cobb Tower, Cessna 5–6–2–Mike–Papa, holding short of 2–7, request left closed traffic."*

TWR – *"Cessna 5–6–2–Mike–Papa, Cobb Tower, left closed traffic approved, runway 2–7 cleared for takeoff."*

PILOT – *"Runway 2–7 cleared for takeoff, Cessna 5–6–2–Mike Papa."*

EXAMPLE 5 (departing–with instructions)

PILOT – *"Cobb Tower, Cessna 5–6–2–Mike–Papa, holding short of 2–7, request left downwind departure."*

TWR – *"Cessna 5–6–2–Mike–Papa, Cobb Tower, maintain runway heading until advised, runway 2–7 cleared for takeoff."*

PILOT – *"Maintain runway heading, runway 2–7 cleared for takeoff, Cessna 5–6–2–Mike Papa."*

EXAMPLE 6 (departing–with instructions)

PILOT – *"Cobb Tower, Cessna 5–6–2–Mike–Papa, holding short of 2–7, request right downwind departure."*

TWR – *"Cessna 5–6–2–Mike–Papa, Cobb Tower, right turnout approved at or above 2,000, runway 2–7 cleared for takeoff."*

PILOT – *"Right downwind approved at or above 2,000, runway 2–7 cleared for takeoff, Cessna 5–6–2–Mike Papa."*

PHASE II

DEFINITIONS PART II

RADAR SERVICES (AKA "Flight Following") – Flight Following is a service that you would request if you would like to keep in contact with a controller while flying to your destination. The controllers who provide this "radar service" (i.e. TRACON and/or ARTCC) will only provide service for VFR pilots if their IFR traffic—which is their primary concern—isn't too overwhelming. In other words, if they are too busy, they will not be able to provide radar services. However, 9 times out of 10, they will be more than capable of providing radar services.

The controllers will assign you a squawk code in order to specifically identify you on their radar. This will then allow them to advise you of other aircraft in your vicinity, as well as prevent you from entering restricted airspace. Additionally, should an emergency occur, they will be readily available to assist you.

TRACON (AKA "APPROACH/DEPARTURE") – TRACON stands for "Terminal Radar Approach Control." However, we address them on the radio simply as "Approach", or in some instances, "Departure" (on initial contact, when just departing an airport).

Their purpose is to organize traffic in heavily populated areas, such as Los Angeles, New York, Chicago, etc. VFR aircraft are not required to contact approach unless they are requesting services from them or are entering class B or C airspace.

TRACON is organized in various sectors throughout a populated area. Therefore, you can expect to go from one frequency to another in just a few minutes of flying. Each frequency is assigned a "chunk" of airspace and when you are leaving that area, they will "hand you off" (tell you to change the other sectors' frequency) to the next controller.

ARTCC (AKA "CENTER") – ARTCC stands for Air Route Traffic Control Center. We address them simply as "Center" (e.g., "LA Center" or "Cleveland Center", etc.). ARTCC operates very much like TRACON, except they cover the sparsely populated areas. ARTCC covers the areas primarily used for en–route traffic, where not many departures and arrivals occur.

FSS (AKA "RADIO") – FSS stands for Flight Service Station. They provide two services: handling flight plans and providing weather briefings. You can call them in the air via various frequencies that can be found on the aeronautical charts, or on the ground via their universal phone number (800–WX–BRIEF).

FLIGHT PLANS – Flight plans are a detailed description of a flight to be taken. VFR pilots are encouraged to file and open/activate flight plans once airborne. The flight plan serves as a safety net should the pilot encounter an emergency situation en–route and be out of communication with anyone. Once a flight plan is opened/activated, and should the pilot not close it upon arrival, FSS will then begin doing all possible to locate the pilot/airplane. If they are unsuccessful, they will then dispatch search and rescue within a few hours after the proposed time of arrival.

WEATHER BRIEFINGS – FSS also provides 3 different types of weather briefings (standard, abbreviated, and outlook), which details weather regarding a specified flight plan.

APPROACH (TRACON)/CENTER (ARTCC)

Getting Flight Following (i.e. Radar Services) is a highly recommended practice when flying a long trip. The benefits include traffic awareness (other airplanes), airspace awareness, some weather information, etc. In addition, Approach or Center can help during emergencies.

It is important to remember that Approach/Departure Control and Center both provide the exact same service. Simply, one of them (Center) covers a much larger area, whereas Approach/Departure covers busy terminal areas such as Los Angeles, New York, and Chicago. To eliminate confusion, it is best not to think of them as different entities, but instead as two parts of the same whole.

Radar Service is not just recommended, but it is a required practice when flying into or out of a class B or C airport. Pilots must contact Approach prior to entering class B or C airspace. In the event of going into class B, pilots must be given a specific clearance to enter class B airspace (e.g. "...cleared to enter Las Vegas B airspace...").

The basics of communication still apply with Approach and Center, but during initial contact the information you provide must be a little more detailed. In addition to giving them your call sign, you must also let them know your "type and equipment suffix". For a Cessna 172 with a GPS (C172/G), you would say "Cessna 172 slant golf." The most common equipment used is Alpha, Uniform, and Golf. Refer to the AIM for a list of equipment suffixes.

In regards to receiving Flight Following, pilots must request it in the air with Approach/Departure or Center. When departing a class B or C airport, flight following will be established on the ground with Clearance Delivery (see the Clearance Delivery section for an example). In some instances, when departing certain class D airports (typically those surrounding busy terminal areas), Flight Following can be established with Ground Control. Should the pilot receive a VFR clearance for Flight Following on the ground, he/she can expect to receive the following information: initial route to be flown, initial altitude to maintain, frequency to contact once the tower gives a "hand–off," and a transponder code. Use the "RAFT" mnemonic to copy a VFR clearance on the ground (i.e. route, altitude, frequency, and transponder).

Keep in mind that the priority of Approach/Departure and Center is to handle IFR flights, so getting VFR Flight Following may not always be accessible when ATC is handling an overwhelming amount of aircraft. Sometimes, after the pilot announces he/she has a request, ATC may respond with something like, "Aircraft calling with a VFR request, unable at this time, try back in 5 minutes."

Once Flight Following has been established, there won't be too much communication between the pilot and ATC. However, the pilot must stay vigilant in listening for his/her call sign. Staying with controller can last anywhere between 5–25 minutes. Once exiting the controller's sector, the pilot will be asked to switch to a different controller/frequency. The pilot should read back the frequency and call the new frequency as soon as practicable. Since the pilot is already in the system with his/her squawk code, the new controller will already know all of the vital information (type of aircraft, destination, etc.). The communication with the new controller should include your altitude (e.g. "SoCal Approach, Cessna 5–6–2–Mike–Papa, checking in at niner thousand five hundred.").

ATC PHRASES

There are a few phrases that a pilot will specifically encounter during Flight Following. Refer to the list below to become familiar with the common phrases:

"SAY TYPE AND EQUIPMENT" – ATC is asking you for your type of airplane (e.g. C172, PA28, DA20, etc.) and equipment suffix (e.g. Uniform, Golf, etc.).

"SAY POSITION" – ATC is asking for your position.

"GO AHEAD" – Proceed with your message. Not to be used for any other purpose (e.g. clearances, etc.).

"SQUAWK" – Activate a specific mode or code on the aircraft transponder.

"RADAR CONTACT" – Used by ATC to inform an aircraft that it is identified on the radar display and radar Flight Following will be provided until radar identification is terminated.

"VECTORS" – Vectors are headings that ATC may issue. Typically these are to avoid other traffic in the vicinity. Pilots may also request vectors if they are having problems locating a landmark or their destination.

"RESUME OWN NAVIGATION (AKA, "NAV") – This means you may continue on course as you please. This may be said after ATC had you on vectors.

"MAINTAIN AT OR ABOVE…" – ATC is asking you to maintain at or above a certain altitude.

"MAINTAIN AT OR BELOW…" – ATC is asking you to maintain at or below a certain altitude.

"CANCEL ALTITUDE RESTRICTIONS" – Adherence to previously imposed altitude restrictions is no longer required during a potential climb or descent.

"ALTITUDE YOUR DISCRETION" OR "DESCENT AT YOUR DISCRETION" – ATC is letting you know that you can do whatever you want with your altitude, whether it's stay at the same altitude, climb, or descend. When approaching your destination, this is a cue that a descent should be started soon.

"PILOT'S DISCRETION" – When used in conjunction with altitude assignments, means that ATC has offered the pilot the option of starting climb or descent whenever he/she wishes and conducting the climb or descent at any rate he/she wishes.

"REPORT AIRPORT IN SIGHT" OR "AIRPORT IS 12 O'CLOCK, 10 MILES…" – ATC is asking you to report when you have the airport in sight. Sometimes ATC will inform you of the airport location. Pilots should respond just like they would for a traffic report.

"I HAVE NO LANDING OR WEATHER INFORMATION FOR ABC AIRPORT…" – ATC will say this when they have no information on your destination. They will usually say this when you are approaching your destination and your destination airport is uncontrolled.

"ADVISE WHEN YOU HAVE THE CURRENT WEATHER AT ABC" OR "INFORMATION CHARLIE IS CURRENT AT ABC" – When your destination airport has ATIS and you are approaching it, ATC will advise you of the current ATIS information. In other words, they are asking you to get the current ATIS information. Pilots are requested to advise ATC when they have received this information.

"HAVE THE NUMBERS" – Used by pilots to inform ATC that they have received runway, wind, and altimeter information only. This is especially useful when informing ATC that you have received the weather information at an uncontrolled airport.

"RADAR SERVICE TERMINATED" – They have ended radar services. Though not always the case, this usually occurs when you are near your destination.

"SQUAWK 1200" OR "SQUAWK AND MAINTAIN VFR" – ATC is asking you to squawk 1200 on your transponder. They will usually say this after they announce, "radar service terminated."

"CHANGE TO ADVISORIES APPROVED" – ATC is allowing you a frequency change to CTAF. This is typically said after ATC announces, "radar services are terminated."

"TRAFFIC ALERT!" – This is a serious warning letting you know that you have an aircraft very near you and a mid–air collision may be imminent.

"HOW DO YOU PLAN TO NAVIGATE?" OR "SAY ROUTE OF FLIGHT" – They want to know what your checkpoints are. They will typically ask this when entering a class B terminal area.

"RADAR CONTACT LOST" – Used by ATC to inform a pilot that radar data used to determine the aircraft's position is no longer being received, or is no longer reliable and radar service is no longer being provided. The loss may be attributed to several factors including the aircraft merging with weather or ground clutter, the aircraft operating below radar coverage, the aircraft entering an area of poor radar reception, failure of the aircraft transponder, or failure of radar equipment.

"UNABLE" – Indicates inability to comply with a specific instruction, request, or clearance.

OBTAINING RADAR SERVICES ("FLIGHT FOLLOWING")

Because the priority of Approach and Center is to handle IFR traffic, VFR pilots should initially advise ATC that they have a request. If ATC has the time, which they usually do, they will ask you to go ahead with your request.

EXAMPLE 1

PILOT – *"SoCal Approach, Cessna 5–6–2–Mike–Papa, with a VFR request."*

ATC – *"Cessna 5–6–2–Mike–Papa, SoCal Approach, say type, equipment, and destination*."*

PILOT – *"SoCal Approach, Cessna 5–6–2–Mike–Papa, a Cessna 172 slant golf, over Seal Beach VOR, request flight following to North Las Vegas at niner thousand five hundred."*

ATC – *"Cessna 2–Mike–Papa, standby for a squawk."*

PILOT – *"Roger, Cessna 2–Mike–Papa."*

ATC – *"Cessna 2–Mike–Papa, squawk 4–2–7–6."*

PILOT – *"Roger, squawk 4-2-7-6, 2–Mike–Papa."*

ATC *"Cessna 2–Mike–Papa, radar contact 3 miles East of Seal Beach, say altitude."*

PILOT – *"Roger, leaving seven thousand two hundred for niner thousand five hundred, 2–Mike–Papa."*

ATC – *"Roger."*

EXAMPLE 2

PILOT – *"SoCal Approach, Cessna 5–6–2–Mike–Papa, with a VFR request."*

ATC – *"Cessna 5–6–2–Mike–Papa, SoCal Approach, go ahead with your request"*

PILOT – *"SoCal Approach, Cessna 5–6–2–Mike–Papa, a Cessna 172 slant golf, South of Ontario, request flight following to Williams Gateway, India Whiskey Alpha (this is the airport identifier, which is not always required), at niner thousand five hundred."*

ATC – *"Cessna 5–6–2–Mike–Papa, squawk 4–2–5–6."*

PILOT – *"Squawk 4–2–5–6, Cessna 5–6–2–Mike–Papa."*

ATC – *"Cessna 2–Mike–Papa, radar contact, 6 miles South of Ontario, Ontario altimeter two niner niner four."*

PILOT – *"Roger, two niner niner four, 2–Mike–Papa."*

EXAMPLE 3

PILOT – *"SoCal Approach, Cessna 5–6–2–Mike–Papa, with a VFR request."*

ATC – *"Cessna 5–6–2–Mike–Papa, SoCal Approach, squawk 0-2-2-5, go ahead with your request"*

PILOT – *"Squawk 0-2-2-5, Cessna 5–6–2–Mike–Papa, a Cessna 172 slant golf, South of Paradise VOR, request flight following to Palm Springs."*

ATC – *"Cessna 2–Mike–Papa, radar contact, 2 miles south of paradise, Ontario altimeter 29.90."*

PILOT – *"Roger, 29.90, 2–Mike–Papa."*

FSS ("RADIO")

Assuming the pilot has already filed a flight plan with Flight Service Station, the pilot should then open the flight plan (typically done just prior to or just after departure). Additionally, a pilot may file a flight plan over the radio, though this can prove to be a daunting task since flight plans are typically very lengthy. Lastly, pilots may utilize "Radio" to obtain weather briefings or to receive PIREPs from pilots.

The frequencies for Flight Service Stations—addressed as "Radio"—vary and can be found on the A/FD and on aeronautical charts. In some cases, the pilot will have to use 2 frequencies, 1 to communicate and 1 to listen to the response. When this is done, the receiving frequency for the pilot will be over a NAVAID, such as a VOR.

PHRASES

"TRANSMITTING ON…" – This phrase is used by pilots to inform FSS the frequency on which he/she is transmitting on.

"RECEIVING ON…" – This phrase is used by pilots to inform FSS the frequency on which he/she is receiving on, since at times, a pilot may transmit on one frequency while receiving on another."

"OPEN/ACTIVATE" – Pilot is requesting FSS to open (AKA "activate") a pre-filed flight plan.

"CLOSE" – Pilot is requesting FSS to close a previously-opened flight plan.

EXAMPLE 1 (Opening/activating a Flight Plan)

PILOT – *"Riverside Radio, Cessna 5–6–2–Mike–Papa, transmitting and receiving on 122.2."*

FSS – *"Cessna 5–6–2–Mike–Papa, Riverside Radio, go ahead."*

PILOT – *"Riverside Radio, Cessna 5–6–2–Mike–Papa, just departed Long Beach and would like to open my flight plan to San Jose at this time*."*

FSS – *"Cessna 2–Mike–Papa, that flight plan is activated, is there anything else I could do for you?"*

PILOT – *"Roger, that will be it, thank you, Cessna 2–Mike–Papa."*

Regardless if the pilot decides to activate the flight plan prior to or after takeoff, the pilot can give FSS a specific time to activate the flight plan (e.g. "...at 1645 Zulu").

EXAMPLE 2 (Closing a Flight Plan)

This can also be done over the phone (800–WX–BRIEF) once the airplane is secured and parked. In this example, the pilot is communicating on 122.6 and using 112.5 to listen to FSS. It will be noted on the aeronautical chart if this technique must be used.

PILOT – *"Riverside Radio, Cessna 5–6–2–Mike–Papa, transmitting on 122.6 and receiving on 112.5."*

FSS – *"Cessna 5–6–2–Mike–Papa, Riverside Radio, go ahead."*

PILOT – *"Riverside Radio, Cessna 5–6–2–Mike–Papa, I would like to close my flight plan to Santa Barbara at this time."*

FSS – *"Cessna 2–Mike–Papa, that flight plan is now closed, have a good day."*

PILOT – *"Roger, thanks, have a great day, Cessna 2–Mike–Papa."*

UNICOM

UNICOM

Universal Communication (UNICOM) is an air to ground communication facility operated by a non-air traffic control private agency to provide an advisory service at uncontrolled airports. UNICOM may also provide various non-flight services, such as taxi instructions and parking information, even at towered airports.

In some cases, the ground station is not staffed, and attempts to communicate will, of course, receive no acknowledgement. During these times, pilots self-announce their position and/or intentions over the CTAF frequency, which is often the same as the UNICOM frequency.

UNICOM EXAMPLES

EXAMPLE 1 – Requesting Airport Advisories
PILOT – *"Weiser UNICOM, Cessna 5–6–2–Mike–Papa, 10 miles South, inbound to land, request airport advisories."*

EXAMPLE 2 – Requesting Parking Information
PILOT – *"Catalina UNICOM, Cessna 5–6–2–Mike–Papa, just landed, requesting parking information."*

EXAMPLE 3 – Requesting Fuel
PILOT – *"Whiteman UNICOM, Cessna 5–6–2–Mike–Papa."*

UNICOM – *"Cessna 5-6-2-Mike-Papa, this is Whiteman UNICOM."*

PILOT – *"Whiteman UNICOM, Cessna 5–6–2–Mike–Papa, we're parked at the North West parking, requesting a top off (fuel)."*

APPENDIX A - UNDERSTANDING ATIS

The Automated Terminal Information Service (ATIS) is the weather and airport information recording that is provided by most controlled airports. It is typically updated every hour (usually about 5 minutes prior to the hour) and the code given will usually be alphabetic (e.g. "Alpha", then the next update will be "Bravo", etc.).

Pilots learning to fly should practice copying down ATIS a few times a day in order to become more familiar with the information that is given. This will allow a new pilot the ability of multi-tasking in the air by flying the airplane and copying down all the pertinent ATIS information.

If you are new to flying, try calling the following phone numbers. During normal operating hours, they will directly connect you to the ATIS for said airport. After a couple of minutes, it will automatically end the call.

St. Louis, MO   (636) 532-3213

White Plains, NY   (914) 948-0130

Hartford, CT   (860) 246-5929

The following is ordered in the same manner in which it is given by ATIS:

1. Airport + Code   _____
2. Time: _____
3. Wind: _____
4. Visibility: _____
5. Weather: _____
6. Temp./Dew Point: _____
7. Altimeter: _____
8. IFR Approach: _____
9. Runway in Use: _____
10. NOTAMs: _____
11. Other: _____

NOTE: AWOS and ASOS are very similar to ATISS, so calling the aforementioned numbers will also help with copying down pertinent weather information given by AWOS and ASOS.

APPENDIX B - OTHER TYPES OF COMMUNICATIONS

LOST PROCEDURES

During flight training, student pilots may become disorientated and lost. If this should ever be the case, pilots should attempt to communicate with the nearest facility. This can be done with TRACON/ARTCC, a nearby tower, FSS, and if all else fails, the emergency frequency (121.5).

If this happens, remember the "C" checklist that includes, but is not limited to: Circle (to fix your position), Climb (to get a better view of your surroundings), Crosscheck VORs (to triangulate your position), and Communicate (AKA "confess" your situation and "comply" with the instructions given by ATC).

There is no structured lingo in this situation. Simply advise ATC who you are and inform them that you are lost.

EXAMPLE
PILOT – *"New York Center, Cessna 5–6–2–Mike–Papa."*

ARTCC – *"Cessna 5–6–2–Mike–Papa, New York Center."*

PILOT – *"New York Center, Cessna 5–6–2–Mike–Papa, student pilot, I am lost and I'm en-route to Stewart International."*

ARTCC – *"Cessna 5–6–2–Mike–Papa, New York Center, squawk 0240 and ident."*

PILOT – *"Squawk 0240 and ident, Cessna 5–6–2–Mike–Papa."*

RADIO FAILURE (SQUAWK 7600)

In the even that a pilot has radio failure, there are procedures in place that a pilot should follow. First, the pilot should attempt to troubleshoot the problem. It could be possible that a circuit breaker popped or the volume was accidentally turned all the way down. Once the pilot has attempted to troubleshoot the situation to no avail, a pilot should squawk 7600. This will advise all radar-equipped ATC of your situation (given that your radio failure was not caused by a total electrical failure). Lastly, the pilot should land as soon as practicable.

If the pilot will be flying into a controlled airport, he/she should overfly the airport just above the airspace ceiling limit. If ATC is aware of the situation, they will illuminate light gun signals from the control tower (so be on the lookout!). If overflying the airport does not garner the attention of the control tower, the pilot may opt to descend to an altitude 500-1,000 feet above traffic pattern (this is also important so the pilot can verify the flow of the traffic). If the control tower continues oblivious to the airplane with radio failure, the pilot should attempt to safely enter the traffic pattern, while being vigilant of other traffic. At some point, tower control will realize the situation and begin issuing light gun signals.

A radio failure can be considered as an emergency, and therefore, landing without a light gun signal may be dismissible. If in doubt, pilots should do a low approach, followed by a go-around, and a re-entry of the traffic pattern.

If a pilot with a radio failure opts to land at an uncontrolled airport, the pilot should follow a similar procedure. First, the pilot should overfly the airport to get familiar with wind indicators and also the flow of the traffic. Secondly, the pilot should enter the traffic pattern using extreme caution for other traffic that may be in the vicinity (e.g. in the traffic pattern, taking off, etc.). Lastly, the pilot should appropriately enter the traffic pattern, and land.

COLOR	ON THE GROUND	IN THE AIR
STEADY GREEN	Cleared for Takeoff	Cleared to land
FLASHING GREEN	Cleared to Taxi	Return for landing
STEADY RED	Stop	Give way to other aircraft
FLASHING RED	Taxi Clear of Runway	Airport unsafe, do not land
FLASHING WHITE	Return to Starting Point	Not applicable
ALTERNATING RED/GREEN	*Exercise extreme caution!*	

In the case that the radio appears to be on and functioning, yet no response is heard from ATC, pilots should use the following terminology:

"TRANSMITTING IN THE BLIND" – A transmission from one station (controller or pilot) to another station (controller or pilot) in circumstances where two–way communication cannot be established, but where it is believed that the called station may be able to receive the transmission.

EMERGENCIES (SQUAWK 7700)

Emergencies can be a daunting situation for any pilot, and effective communication can be the difference between survival and the alternative to survival (for lack of better words). If there is any frequency that a pilot should memorize, it should be 121.5 (just like memorizing 9-1-1). This frequency is monitored by FSS, TRACON/ARTCC, control towers, and the majority of airborne airliners.

Should a pilot encounter a scenario where an emergency should be declared, he/she should contact 121.5. However, if a pilot is already in communication with a Tower, TRACON ("approach"), or ARTCC ("center") or a control tower, then declaring an emergency with them would make more sense, since they are already familiar with your flight situation and location.

Upon experiencing an emergency situation, the pilot should focus on flying and maintaining the safety of flight. As soon as practicable, he/she should declare an emergency and squawk 7700. Declaring an emergency over the radio should be specific to the situation so that the controller can help you as much as they can and also to begin sending help (e.g. the fire department, etc.).

When declaring an emergency, the pilot should advise the controller(s) of the following items:
1. Declaration of the emergency (i.e. "Mayday! Mayday! Mayday!")
2. Aircraft ID (E.g. "Cessna N123AB")
3. Location
4. Emergency situation (e.g. engine failure, fire, etc.)
5. Fuel on board (in time, not gallons—"2 hours of fuel on board")
6. Number of people on board (AKA "souls on board")

HELICOPTER OPERATIONS

The following terminology applies only to rotorcraft.

"TAXI" – This is only issued to wheeled helicopters.

"HOVER TAXI" – A brisk walking speed, 3-5 feet above the ground. Typically it is over taxiways, but a pilot can request direct hover taxi to a specific location on the airport.

"AIR TAXI" – Unlike a hover taxi, which is slow and low, an air taxi is usually flown at 60 knots and 100 feet AGL.

SPECIAL VFR

Pilots may request "special VFR" from a control tower if the weather falls below basic VFR weather minimums (i.e. 3 statute miles and 1,000 foot ceiling). Doing so will allow pilots to navigate to an airport with lower minimums of 1 statute mile and clear of clouds. However, student pilots are NOT allowed to request special VFR without a flight instructor on board. Furthermore, if a Private Pilot wishes to request special VFR at night, that pilot must be Instrument Rated and the aircraft flown must be IFR-equipped.

Requesting Special VFR is very similar to basic pilot/tower communications.

EXAMPLE
PILOT – *"Teterboro tower, Cessna 5–6–2–Mike–Papa, 7 miles West of the field, request special VFR inbound with ATIS information Charlie."*

TOWER – *"Cessna 5–6–2–Mike–Papa, Teterboro Tower, squawk 0-2-2-4."*

PILOT – *"Squawk 0-2-2-4, Cessna 5–6–2–Mike–Papa."*

TOWER – *"Cessna 5–6–2–Mike–Papa, radar contact 6 miles West, cleared to enter class Delta airspace special VFR, make right traffic runway 24."*

PILOT – *"Cleared to enter class Delta airspace special VFR, make right traffic runway 24, Cessna 5–6–2–Mike–Papa."*

Best of luck with your training!!